I0108509

All Gone

A collection of poetry by Abraham Ross
Fourthross.com

Illustrations by Kristen Jussila
Kristen-jussila.com

Fourth

Ross

Copyright © 2016 Abraham Ross
All rights reserved.
ISBN: 0692762639
ISBN-13: 978-0692762639

AUTHORS NOTE

When I was writing one of these poems, a fly landed on my crotch and died.

…no refunds.

Sleeping Atlas

I'll eat up the rain
slapping and slipping down the roof
of that beat up car I was so sure
wouldn't live a week.
The feeling of waxed wood, holding the weight of my arms
while I have my second cup and smile at that
girl in the cafe, kind enough to smile back.
That flint spark, late beyond night; igniting the air in an
overtired mind, when I remember
It would only take twenty minutes to get to the beach.
Favorite words that sound like simple syrup
no matter how many times they're said
over and over, *epoch, brood, epoch, brood*
with *pentameter* thrown in for good measure.
This tug of minutes, swinging the vignettes,
the fickle fourth legged house pet
in and out of the screen door.
Sometimes it's hard to remember
why I live so angrily.

No pastry preserves its sweetness
nor should hands keep from cracking
There's no such lies with the passing
of time, but the indulgent resignation
a fragile smile, held with care.
and the prayer: *please don't blink,*
I'm happy.

This Town

The town in which I live
is the boy behind the school
who didn't think
it was enough
to throw me into the fence

it's not satisfied
only pulling teeth
and telling them
they're better off
that way

it's not finished
never finished
flexing
reminding me
I don't belong here

it finds nothing funnier

I've wrinkles in my skin
from the sweeping tide
missed opportunities
and conversations
turned violent

This town will be
my end

Bedroom Ceiling

Pessimists don't make good lovers.
I can tell because when you smiled at me
On my forest green bed
You didn't get it,
the way I look at this town.
The weeping willows,
the one-way streets,
the student cycling hands-free
entangled in his phone's blue-rimmed future obituary
begging for an audience through solipsis.

My dirt-tinted glasses should have been explained
to you before the night you told me that
You were right for me,
If I'd just give you a chance.

I'm rampant with myself
and you're looking at these stripes of absolution
like you've made a difference.
I have so little to offer, and so much to take,
returned from my sleeve and far out of reach,
you might as well be next to a mannequin.

I thought it would be different.
But the door is closed, and I want you out.

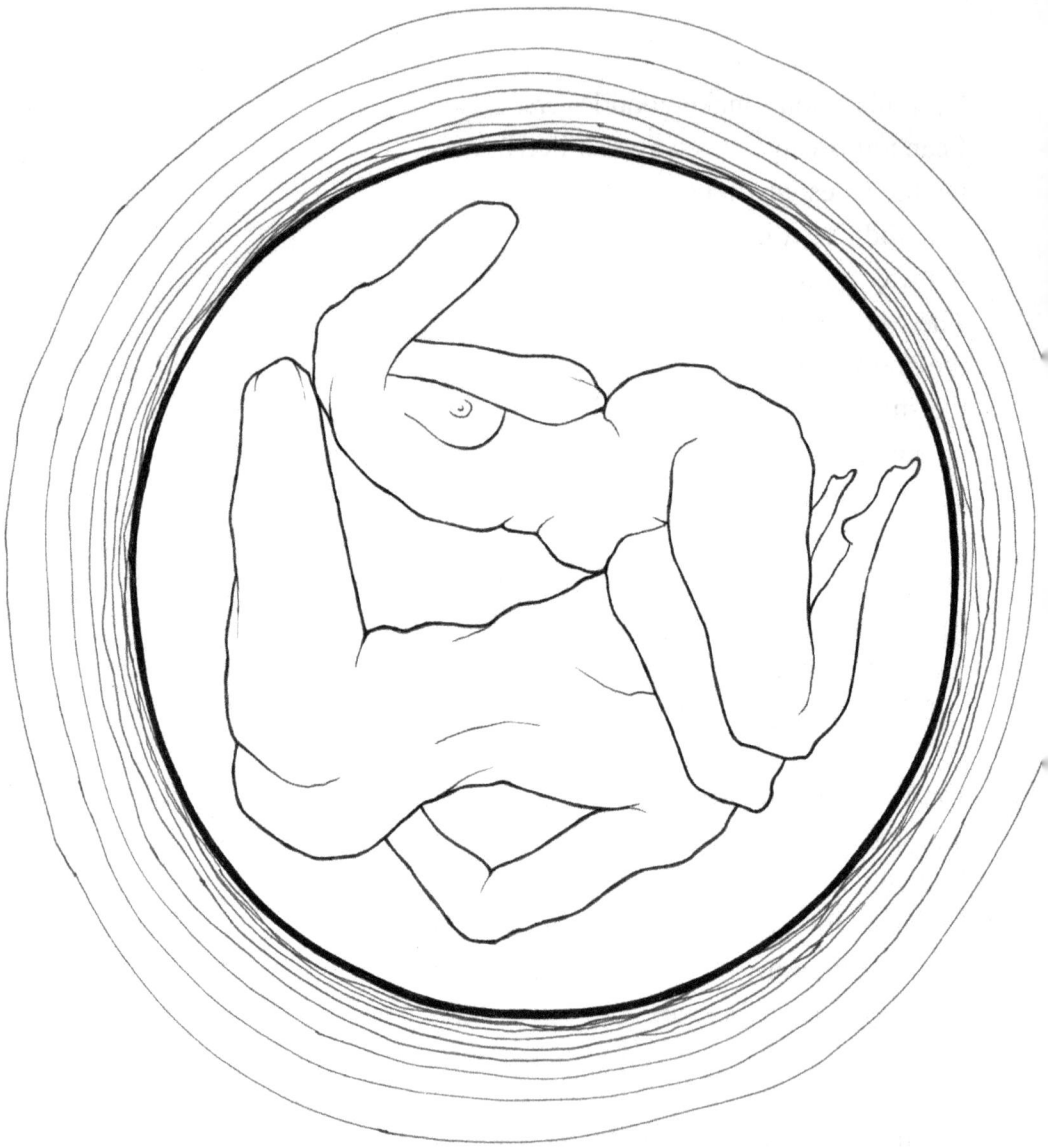

Apnea

When we fall asleep
our bodies still know how to love one another.
My arms won't remember
when they swallow you
that you stopped at every light
and every bar
on your way home.

The light I left on for you
burnt out weeks ago,
but the moon hates to see us apart.
The tide sweeps you back.

I hate the moon,
and your leftover affection.

I want to fly around the world
and have the best day of my life
and realize it's a dream
and realize I don't care.
I want to wake up just enough
to kiss your cheek and bite your neck
and forget why the sound of your car
reaching our driveway
makes me sick.

When we fall asleep
my heart presses against your back
and I could swear you remember
why you loved me once.

For William McMaster Murdoch

My moment of clarity
is in this pocket of snow
I made when I sat down
at four in the morning.

Kindness doesn't belong here.

When I climb back in the
bedroom window,
my shadow of benevolence
will stay outside
where it belongs.

Until then,
I'll catch the matinee
across the fence,
The Broken Family.
testing their windows
with plates or words or looks
and closing each blind
to know the distance
between them

and us.

The lines are busy with bitter speculation,
and their ship is capsizing.

I heard he hits her. Drinks too much,
fucks other women.
I heard that someone
saw him one day
in the city with a woman
what if

I want to be different,
but my mouth is only holding my tongue
because it's too cold out here
to break free.

I want to return my ticket,
this is infectious
and I can't swim.

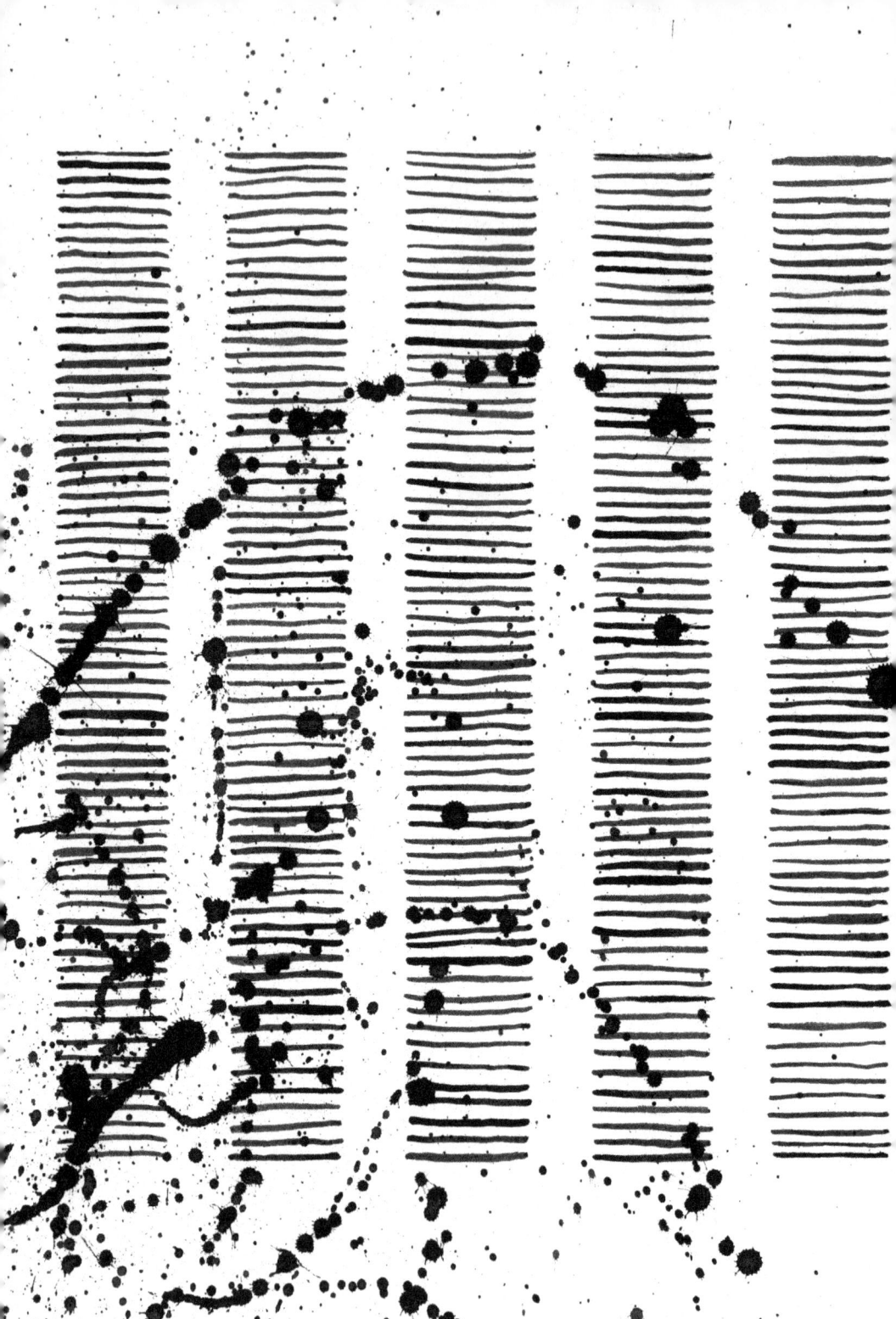

Driftwood

From the moment
I feel like waking
I've lost all of my things
and I know by the time
I collect them all
I'll be hungry again
and I'll be inside another hour

time moves too fast when I'm on
my couch

I'm just the driftwood

I'm swelling and cracking
after every meal
bending with every slap of water

I'm joining the wall
and my bones are screaming to move

this thing with a face
that brings me my drug
It tells me my friends are all having fun
their relationship status has changed
they have thoughts on this and that
and all of them are important enough
to throw out

All Gone

I am alone
I am indifferent
I'm pretending to sleep
I'm not lonely enough
I don't want to settle
I don't want my life
to be about someone
else
I don't want to be boring
I don't want to be boring
I don't want to be boring
I don't want to be boring
going out is empty
and cheap
where we go isn't cheap
no one is having fun
until we spend money
on drinks
or time
on cigarettes
half of us are just here
to fulfill the hope
and the other half are
just as bland
talking about
politics
or
that funny story
about the time we had sex
with someone
I'm listening

it never gets old
but I'm tired
thinking about sex
I've got to have sex
I've got to have good sex.
I've got to have really good sex
if I don't, I'm alone
I'm
alone
no one's counting
everyone is having fun
this is work
this is shit
I don't understand
I don't want to be
awake
I'm all gone
I'm listening to
Modern family
on my computer
everything on tv
is a kodak moment
everything in this house
isn't.

Love is Useless

I'm hungry
but eating will make things messy,
and I'm tired of cleaning.

Standing in the kitchen
at some time that isn't normal,
staring at the egg-drop soup.
Steaming in the black bin,
The pot it scrambled in is too ugly
to look at.

I could fill my stomach with
something simple.
Blueberry bagels and leftover chips,
but I'm so bored,
and the ice cream in my freezer
will only leave me
wanting more.

I'm going to bed hungry.
I was never good at this sort of thing.

Epoch

On the edge of everything
where the waves brush
and drag the sand
to the great deep
all we've ever felt
is lost
in the black water

the ageless colossus
rises to the moon each night
and returns to its bed
awaiting the day it will
swallow us
and our bitterness

wash the red from our hands
and our kind from this home
and the world will breathe again
with echoes of hymns
and we'll earn back our love
with the hope of absolution.

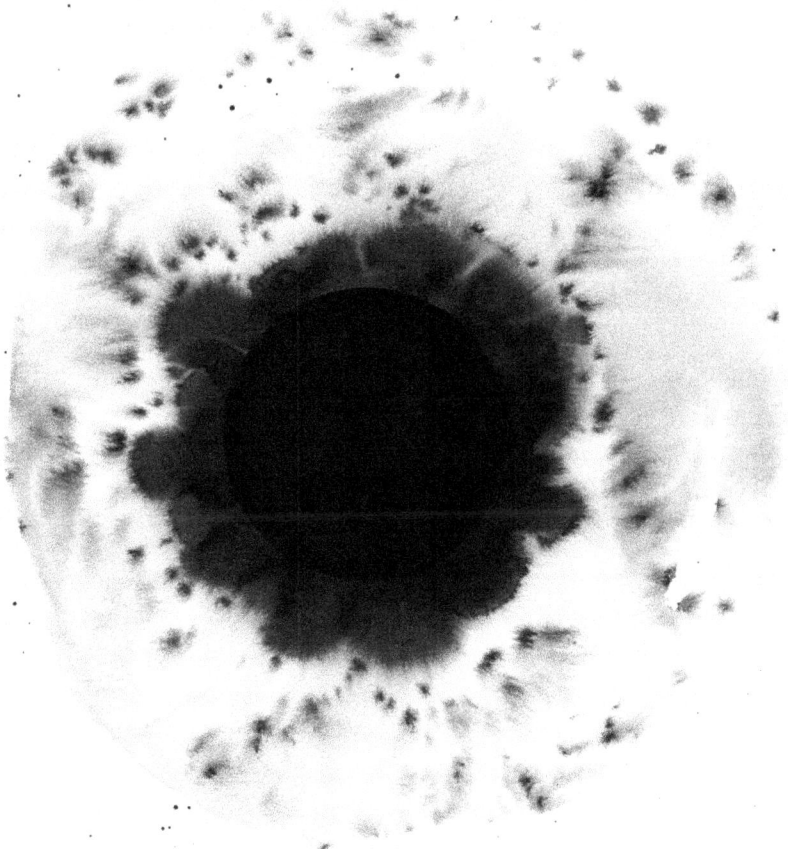

Morning Routine

I can't swim
the growing seventy one
percent
of the world
would fill my lungs
happily
and drag me back
into the chain of things
and tumors could be growing
inside of me, and we get
diseases from sleeping
with one another
but sex still sells
better than condoms
and there's a fungus
that's grown
two thousand acres
underground
that can poison
threatening plants
and humans kill
humans
and talk about it on
a screen to other humans
to reassure them
those ones are in a box together
and I drank water out of a cup
I didn't know had curdled
milk at the bottom.

When I Have Nothing Else

A girl once told me I was dead
to her and then kept using
my Netflix account.
I wonder if she thought
she was haunted when I
cancelled it.

I don't know how everyone
swallows cheap love like
half-cooked meat
ready to turn
in their stomach and make them
sick for days
things change in one sentence
and their needle keeps skipping
and no one learns
because loving
means something that
we don't have the patience for
but it's easier to be alone
when you're with someone
than it is
with a mirror.

Effortless

Snow is an agent
wrapping his body
and pulling the stopper
in his lungs
so all he has to do
is sit
and watch his limbs
turn black

somewhere here
on the other side
of the snow cap mountain
there's another
who feels alive
and moves with urgency
to the end of the earth
so that after
he may feel the warmth
he lost over time

when the remaining give in
and say goodbye
to themselves
like an old friend
the snow
kind director
buries them
with a blanket
so they may find warmth
in the comfort of sleep

Tinder Date

Thirty minutes is all it took
for you to wear me
down and we're talking
about the profundity of
needles.
The pigment on my skin has
become an icebreaking trope
and my hopes from sleeves
rolled down have been made
in vain, and suddenly
I'm so
fucking
bored.

Picking my brain has
nothing of value
for me
or for you
and despite the
quality time title
retrospection will
give this paddleboat
I am dead
in the water
reclined and waiting
with a drink in my hand
that isn't as strong
as I'll pretend.

My life is moving slower
than I could tell you
and I'm sorry
because you're trying.
Your voice is sweet
but I don't want it.

I just can't care that you stood in
a room with Joyce Manor
while they played your
favorite song.

Am I this lonely?
Is she?

Gin and Tonic

Somewhere in this bar
beyond the boys
trying desperately
to get the girls drunk
Is the Christian twenty-something
watching them both
empty the trough
he's content
with his final judgment
but damned all the same
because excess is relative
and he's not full yet.

When I've finished my
second drink
and ordered another
I'll find him
on the porch and
watch the corners of his mouth
while he talks.

He'll tell me how
he hates bars
that people act stupid
when they think
everyone likes them
only twice mentioning
that my breath smells of gin.

He knows to be polite
but his words are sharp on both ends
the kind that tell me to hold my tongue
and remember that
while our cups look the same
mine has water spots.

Keyboard Warrior

Armchair activist. Freelance fascist.
Tell me how you think, so you can get back
this
fickle feeling laying on your mattress
tweeting madness
preach to the sheep, your Holy Badness
maybe one day I can reach your level
of pious crass-ness
and you'll speak to me like I'm a god.
Your equal.
I'm full and festering with this collective
circle jerk
this lack of work way of life.
Everyone speaks and spits
their mind like it matters on matters that
flatter their ego till it gets
fatter and fatter
and people die
because that Upworthy post you shared
and boasted awareness for did
nothing.
We're all aware, we all care, just not enough.
Besides, Walking Dead is on!
Consume and go wild, leave that kid
In the cold.
He'll get it when he's grown.
If he didn't want to starve
maybe he should have shared
his *indie lifestyle* on Now This
a few more times.

If it means so much
if that dying mother needs a crutch
They'll make a petition.
If they're lucky, we'll take our hands
off our crotches
to type in our email.

You Were Right

I won't change.
I was lonely before you
and after
the space in between
was no different.

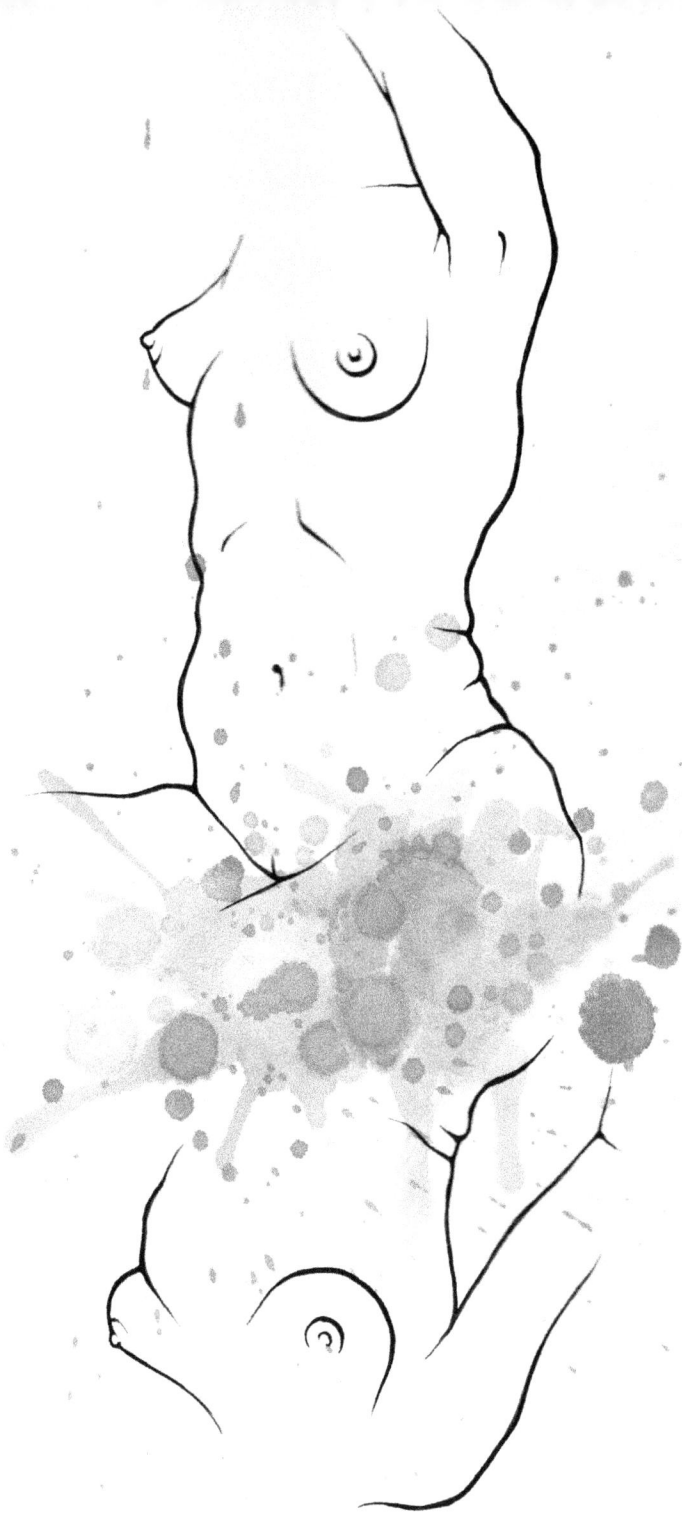

27

Synapses

If our brains had switches
and bulbs
I think most people
would rip the plug
from the wall
on Sunday

the week will be painful
and swollen with regret
people we've hurt
and others we'd like to

before we leap in
the Monday sun
that makes our skin bubble
and cheeks go red
most people will go to church

they'll listen to the words
of a well dressed human
and take what they need
because when the light
in their brain continues to burn
the lie
"You are loved"
will give them shade

Kitchen Sink

I'm the most important person in the world
when you tell me that I'm worthless.
Let's jump and scream until our cheeks grow red,
spent with the soreness of our shaking sides.
I want so badly to sleep but can't close my eyes.
you'll still be looking at me
like that.

I won't ever feel a touch like yours
making up for the names you called me,
or hold someone as if to say
I didn't mean it, I won't leave.

I've been free of you for several months
at least the days.
I still spend the nights, afraid to close
my eyes,
when they do I'll dream you
looking at me
like that.

Nostalgia

I used to talk on my way home
sorting my mess out in twenty minutes
and knowing silence that wasn't
unbearable.

One morning a boy from class
said he saw me walking
from his bus window.
My walks grew quiet
long division became harder
in my head
and today
I still keep staring
at the rocks in front of my feet.

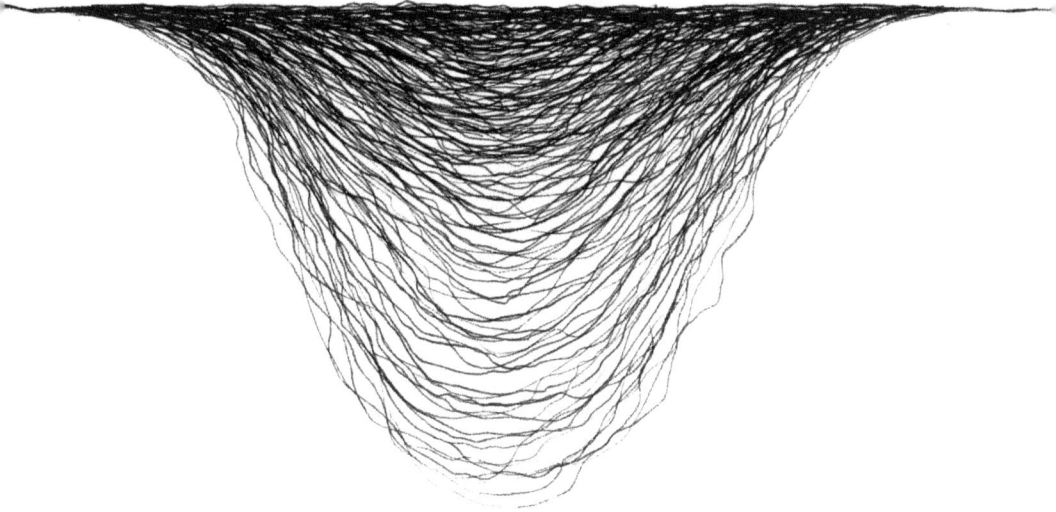

Thumbs

Children with *daddy issues*
often have their father's eyes
reflections to remind
us what we've yet
to do

we've only fought once
about my tattoos

the house shook
and I drove into the city
hoping to stall
only to return
over your stare
in the rearview mirror

I have your thumbs
and hidden temper
white knuckles resting
on my self conscious skin
while I wonder
who you would be
if I looked like someone else

I know I'm lucky
to have been the last
the remainder when the other children
shipped off
I have more of your blood in me
than I could admit
too soft to spill
for any spirit or sickness
so be it

when the great night sweeps you
long down the road
I'll spend weeks in the bathroom
waiting for my reflection to
return your smile
and remind me who I am.

Closed Doors

Pulsing lines in red sand
to the sound of separation
will drown our cry of a
released embrace
suffocating our
comfort and Compassion
with a name tag
simulations of simple voices
rise from our throats and
sit us down with a false sense
of diversity
a world that knows who we are
the color of our blood
the way we love
and the price of our voice

the foundation of our crime
is the consumption of
empty walls
shouting
that we are anything
but the same

Coasting

I'm never drunk until my bike ride home
when I remember
that the things in my bedroom
will be too easy to knock over.

It's hard to talk with someone
who hates you,
when their voice is louder
than the tv's in the bar.

By my arrival
The front steps to my home
will have become fear,
and I'm praying my only friend
in the whitehead of Georgia
is sleeping in his bed
or someone else's
and if he isn't
my own will be one he'll
have to hear about
and it's absurd inhabitance.

I want to go home,
but I can't
and I won't read this
because it doesn't matter what I think
I want to look good
for the girl at my work
who doesn't like me.

Side Effects

People are boring
and so am I
and that new funny picture
of the politician I don't like
isn't clever.

There is no sense of purpose
that can stroll alongside this great
anhedonance.
Love is Pyrrhic
sex is vapid
and work is
investing days for the
drug we can't afford
crawling on our hands and knees
for a placebo life
trembling through the self-driven
mirage of our advertised days
and strangling hope
with our childlike grip
begging for the morning
that we mean something
to someone else
because we still don't know
how to love ourselves.

Tethered

When we ran
to the beaten and
battered mill
breaking in was easy
leaving echoes
and footprints
and I hadn't realized
yet
that the universe was
complete

I'm still starving
long down the road
for something that
I can only taste in
the chorus of
music I play
over and over
I could listen to you talk
until the words are nothing

sometimes I wonder
who makes you
smile now
because change
is beautiful
and you
made me laugh
harder than anyone else

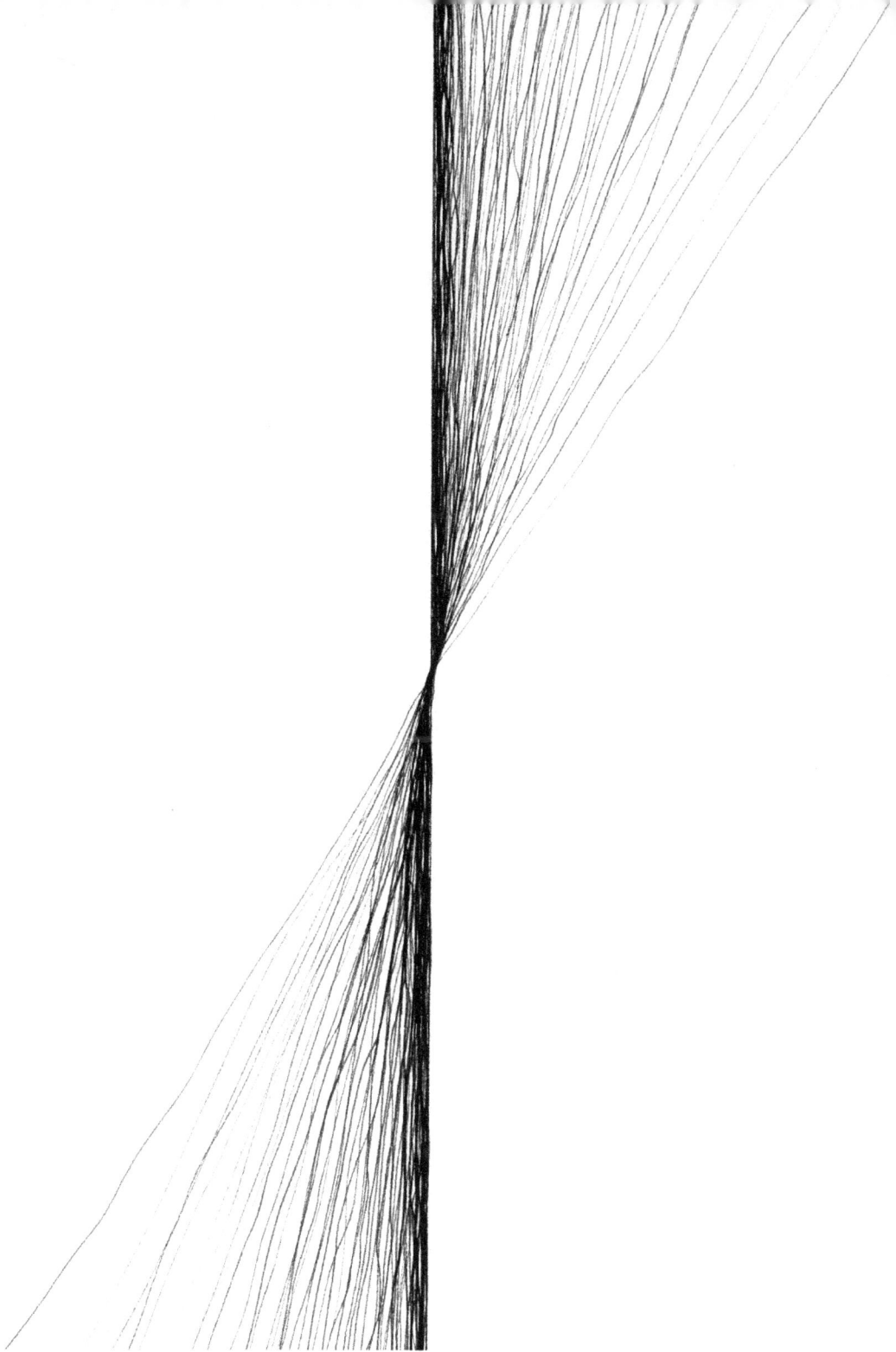

Sight Unseen

Diplomacy fails between my spine and eyes
while I sit on this bench
drinking my coffee
and pretending not to look at the
pretty girl with short hair.

I know,
I'm tired of *writing* this bullshit too.

Fundamental lies I've seen
on Tv screens and actors admissions
of living happily on their pedestal.
this flaking rose, countdown clock
to the white picket strings holding
two people together.

My roommate says that we do this
so that when we sleep
our home is less lonely

I don't fit in
and when I hold someone's hand
I keep my eyes on my feet
waiting for the other shoe
to drop.

If I were different
I think
I wouldn't like
to meet myself.

Silences

'What will make you happy?'
she said with a smirk
I thought was unfair.

She was watching miles
from my thoughts
pretending to understand
every piece of unturned brick.

It's cold in this bathroom
while I talk to myself
and she's outside
with her own intentions
thinking she's earned
some sort of reward.

I want this house empty
the loose chairs to be
scraped and thrown out
I want nothing but bare
wooden floors
to lie down on
and feel like once again
I have something else to work on
than myself.

Used Car Salesman

Your love is two-dollar wine
leaving my stomach unsure
for your 'friendship'

this straight and narrow route
this heartsick
cultivation
this balance beam
you've set is shaking
while you wait below
with open arms
as if you hadn't kicked
the base.

I'm not your
puzzle to solve or some
tattooed-hipster muse.
my problems are boring
and you've seen no side of me.
Our life isn't a film
and your *will they, won't they*
way of talking is just
taxing.

When you work me over in
your heart's clichés
and your lifelike structure
I'm a badly written side plot
in the self rewarding memoir
you will never write.

Can't you just tell me what you want,
so I can tell you that I don't have it?

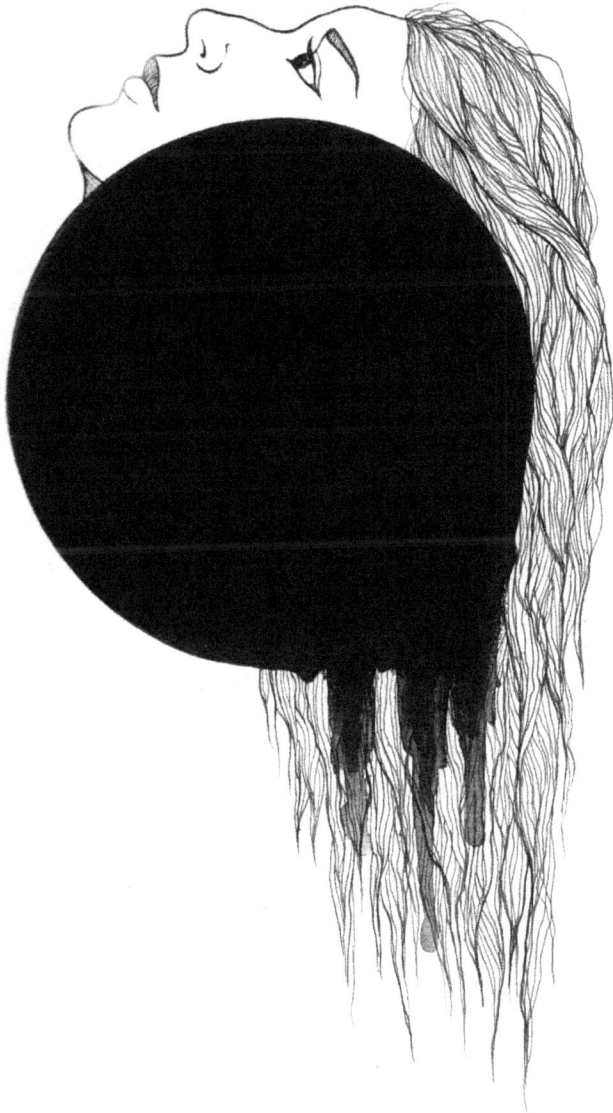

The Taste of Copper

My mind is leaving me to deal
with myself
until my teeth rot
and pupils flake
and she's abstracted

I'll leave these pennies face up
so luck will work backwards
and I'll think she didn't flourish
when he touched her shoulders

I've grown
tangible and jealous
hearing the second-hand
bitterness of the
boys devoured
while she fought and hit and bit
the neck of anyone
I could imagine
that love is in the air

I wonder if she still smokes
floating
down her great stagnation
pressing more names
into a bruising mold
and growing tired
as I am
of thinking about her

www.ingramcontent.com/pod-product-compliance
Lightning Source LLC
Chambersburg PA
CBHW061844040426
42447CB00012B/3130